EVERY DROP COUNTS

A Book About Water

By  Jill Wheeler

Illustrations by Angela Kamstra
and
Kristi Schaeppi

Published by Abdo & Daughters, 4940 Viking Drive suite 622, Edina, Minnesota 55435

Library bound edition distributed by Rockbottom Books, Pentagon Towers, P.O. Box 36036, Minneapolis, Minnesota 55435.

Interior photograph - Stock Market

Edited by Julie Berg

LIBRARY OF CONGRESS CATALOGING-IN-PUBLICATION DATA
Wheeler, Jill C., 1964 -
    Every drop counts : a book about water / written by Jill Wheeler.
        p.   cm. -- (Target earth)
    Summary: Discusses water conservation and suggests ways we can safeguard this precious resource.
    ISBN 1-56239-195-X
    1. Water conservation -- Juvenile literature. 2. Water -- Pollution -- Juvenile literature. [1. Water conservation. 2. Water -- Pollution. 3. Pollution.] I. Title. II. Series.
    TD38.W47 1993
    363.73'946525--dc20
    [B]   93-15463
                                      CIP
                                      AC

Thanks To The Trees From Which This Recycled Paper Was First Made.

Table of Contents

Let's Begin Here.

Water is our most precious resource. More than 65 percent of our bodies are water. People can survive without water only a few days. All living things would die if they didn't have water.

We use water many ways. We use it for drinking and washing. We use it for cleaning our clothes and homes. We use it for growing and cooking food. In the United States, each person uses about 60 gallons (227 liters) of water a day.

In addition, factories use water for making their products. Power companies use water to generate electricity. People use water to transport themselves and the products they use.

Our water resources are *finite*. That means we have only what we have now. We cannot create more. Of all the water on Earth, only 1 percent is drinkable. Ninety-seven percent of our water is in the oceans. That water is saltwater and we cannot drink it. Other water is frozen near the North and South Poles.

About 3 percent of the water on Earth is fresh water which we drink. The rest is saltwater. A person can only live a few days without water.

Drinking water comes from only a few places. It comes from surface waters, such as rivers and lakes. It comes from underground reservoirs called *aquifers*. More than 95 percent of our water comes from aquifers. This water is called *groundwater*.

People must be careful of the water they drink. Polluted water can look like pure water. Many pollutants are invisible chemicals. Sometimes these chemicals cannot be tasted or smelled. This causes many problems. People can get sick drinking water that seems pure.

It's easy to see why water is so precious. It's also easy to see why we must be concerned. Polluted water helps no one. Clean water helps everyone.

In this book, we will see how people are polluting water. We'll see how that *pollution* affects us. We'll find out what we can do to help stop it.

The First Drops

The water we drink is as old as the Earth. That makes it about 4.5 billion years old. Our water has been used by many other people, animals and plants before us.

Scientists aren't sure how water was created. Many believe water was at the Earth's center billions of years ago. It was very hot inside the Earth then. It was so hot the water was in its vapor form. That form is called steam. The steam came to the surface through breaks in the Earth's crust. These breaks are called *volcanoes, geysers* and *hot springs*.

Things changed about one million years ago. The Earth's climate became much colder. The water froze into giant sheets of mile-thick ice. These were called *glaciers*. The glaciers moved slowly across the land. They created the landscape we know today.

Then the Earth began to warm. The glaciers melted. Lakes formed in the holes the glaciers had scraped. Other water created the oceans. Rainwater soaked into the Earth. It became groundwater.

Glaciers were formed about one million years ago. They still exist today in beautiful landscapes such as these.

Water from the glaciers was very clean. It had only some soil and plant material in it. The water was not harmful to living things.

Water pollution began with people. People dumped their waste into rivers and oceans. It was easy for them to dump their waste there.

At first, the dumping was not a problem. There was not enough waste to harm anyone. Then more people lived on the Earth. There was more waste in the water. The polluted water began to harm people, animals and plants.

The water pollution problem became worse. People began dumping harmful chemicals into the water. These chemicals are called *toxins*. There are many kinds of toxins. There are toxins in herbicides and pesticides. They are in oil and household cleaners. Sometimes people accidentally eat or drink something with toxins in it. They often get sick. Some people even die.

People began to learn about toxins in water in the late 1950s. It happened around Minamata Bay in Japan. Many of the people who lived near the bay began to get sick. Some lost control of their arms and legs. Others went deaf and blind. Still others died.

Doctors discovered the people had *mercury* poisoning. They learned a nearby factory was dumping wastes into the water. These wastes included mercury. Fish had eaten the mercury. Then people ate the fish and became sick.

Mercury is a heavy metal. *Cadmium* and *lead* are two other heavy metals. People get sick if heavy metals get into their bodies. The metals can even cause brain damage. These metals get into the body through air, food and water. Heavy metals also can harm children before they are born.

Minamata Bay is one of many places that has had problems with toxins. In the United States, Cleveland, Ohio, had a problem, too. In June 1969, a river near Cleveland burst into flames. The river is called the Cuyahoga River. Normally water cannot burn. It is used to put out fires. The Cuyahoga burned because it was full of pollutants. Factories near the Cuyahoga had dumped many pollutants into the river. The pollutants included oil, which burns easily. The river fire caused a lot of damage.

Ten years later, there was a problem in the Love Canal neighborhood of Niagara, New York. Thousands of residents had to leave their homes. They discovered people had buried *hazardous waste* in their neighborhood. The waste *contaminated* their water for more than 20 years. The bad water made people in that neighborhood sick.

The people had higher than normal *cancer* rates. Many of the women had *miscarriages*. Some of the children born in the neighborhood had *birth defects*.

In November 1987, disaster struck people in Pennsylvania and West Virginia. A huge diesel fuel spill contaminated the Monongahela River. Thousands of people had to buy bottled water to drink. In 1989, a terrible oil spill happened in Prince William Sound in Alaska. The *Exxon Valdez* supertanker dumped 11 million gallons (42 million liters) of crude oil into the Sound. The oil killed thousands of fish, birds and other wildlife. Ugly black oil sludge washed up on the shore.

These are just a few examples of water pollution. There are many other places that have polluted water. People discover new water pollution almost every day. In the next chapter, we will see why.

An average of 425 oil spills and 75 chemical spills occur every month in the Great Lakes.

"Current" Conditions

In 1988, a *drought* hit many parts of the United States. A drought is when there is not enough rain. This drought was the worst in more than 50 years. Grass, trees and shrubs withered and died. People and animals suffered in the heat. Some of them died. Many people wondered if there would ever be enough water again.

That drought ended in the early 1990s. Yet it made many people think about the water they drink. The drought made people realize clean, drinkable water is precious. They realized more people means more demand for water. Yet the number of people is always growing. The water supply never grows.

In the United States, we use about 450 billion gallons (1.7 trillion liters) of water each day. Most of that water comes from surface waters and aquifers. Sadly, it is easy to harm both of these water sources.

We harm the water we drink when we spray *pesticides* on our lawns. We harm it when we dump hazardous wastes on the ground. These wastes include motor oil, paints and household chemicals. All of these pollutants filter down through the soil. Eventually the pollutants reach the aquifers.

Did You Know...

One quart of
motor oil can
poison 250,000
gallons (946,000
liters) of water.

Did You Know...

In just one minute you waste a gallon of water when you turn the faucet on full-blast.

We harm our water when we send garbage to *landfills*. Garbage can contain harmful chemicals. These chemicals seep through the ground in the landfill. They end up in groundwater. One landfill can do a lot of damage to nearby water supplies. It can leak up to four million gallons (15 million liters) of toxic liquids a day.

We harm the water we drink when we operate appliances which run on electricity. Power plants use water to cool their equipment. When the plants return the water, it is much warmer. Warm water cannot hold as much oxygen as cool water. This oxygen shortage harms the fish and plants that live in the water. Warm water also encourages *bacteria*, which makes people sick.

We harm the water when we use paper, steel and chemicals. We harm it when we use processed food and man-made fabrics. The industries that make these products are among the worst polluters. When they make them, they create waste. Then they dump the waste into the water. The waste includes oil, acids, metal and wood chips. It also includes animal parts, dyes, salt and plastics. These industries also use a lot of water to manufacture these goods. Water helps them make electricity, and cool and clean equipment.

Did You Know...

We lose between 50 and 80 percent of the water we put on our lawns. Some is lost to evaporation. Some seeps into the ground. Some runs off into the street.

We harm our water when we over-water our lawns. We harm it when we wash our cars every week. We harm it when we leave the water running in the sink. All of these activities waste water. Remember, we only have 1 percent to use!

We harm our water when we flush wastes down the toilet. Believe it or not, it's legal to dump some wastes into the ocean. People legally dump more than 189 million tons (171 billion kilograms) of solid waste into the oceans each year. The waste comes from pipes called *ocean outfalls*. These drain sewage directly into the ocean. Sewage comes from drains and toilets.

We harm our water when we buy food grown with agricultural chemicals. We harm it when we buy food produced on irrigated land or drained *wetlands*. Agricultural chemicals are substances like pesticides, *herbicides* and *fertilizers*. These chemicals can wash off farmland. They can wash into groundwater and contaminate it. Irrigation systems drain away scarce water. Draining wetlands to create farmland also hurts our water. Wetlands clean our water. They filter *sediment* and trap harmful chemicals. America is losing wetlands rapidly. We lose about 300,000 acres (121,000 hectares) of wetlands per year.

People are doing many things to harm the water we drink. There are many things we can do to help, too. We can pitch in to clean dirty water and *conserve* clean water. The next chapter shows how.

Did You Know...

The price of water has jumped in recent years. It's increased as much as 37 percent in some U.S. cities.

Make Waves about Water Waste! 3

Everyone can conserve water and reduce water pollution every day. All you have to do is follow a few simple steps. Read on for some water-saving ideas:

Save The Water at Home

Don't leave the water running when you brush your teeth. Don't leave it running when you wash dishes or food. Use a tub of soapy water to wash dishes. Then turn the faucet on halfway to rinse. You waste water when you turn the faucet on full-blast. You can waste a whole gallon (3.8 liters) in just 60 seconds that way.

💧 Don't use the kitchen sink as a dump. Everything you send down the drain may go to a water treatment plant. Then it may end up back in your faucet. These are substances like household cleaners and paint. If you do use them, store them in tightly closed containers. When you're through with them, take them to a hazardous waste collection point.

💧 Put a quart bottle filled with water in your toilet tank. You'll use less water per flush. One bottle can reduce your water use 15 percent each day.

💧 Keep a bottle of drinking water in the refrigerator. Then you won't have to run the faucet until the water's cold.

💧 Watch what you eat. It takes 2,500 gallons (9,462 liters) of water to produce one pound of beef. It takes 408 gallons (1,544 liters) of water to produce a serving of chicken. Vegetables take much less water to produce.

💧 Have your parents check your detergents for *phosphates*. Phosphates kill lakes and streams. Phosphates encourage algae and bacteria to grow. Use low-phosphate or phosphate-free detergents. Most soap packages tell if the detergent is phosphate-free. Use less detergent overall. Many detergent manufacturers tell you to use more than you need.

Did You Know...

One leaky faucet can waste over fifty gallons (190 liters) of water a day.

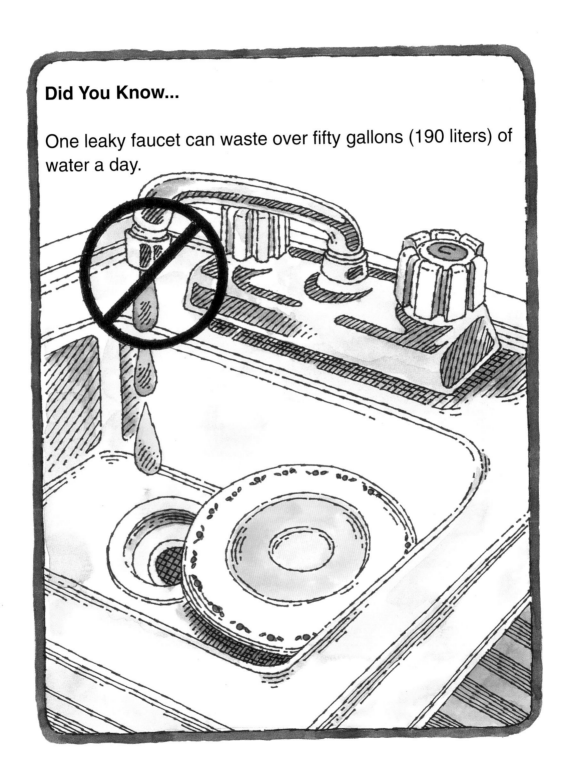

Clean *latex*-paint-filled brushes indoors. This way the wastewater can go to a water treatment facility. Don't clean brushes outside. The waste goes into the ground then.

Fix leaks. One leaky faucet can waste over 50 gallons (190 liters) of water a day. A leaky toilet wastes 750 gallons (2,800 liters) of water a month.

Recycle. Then there will be less garbage going to the landfill. The less garbage, the less chance toxins will leak into the water.

Take a shower instead of a bath. Showers use one-third less water than baths.

Did You Know...

Toilets use 40 percent of all household water. Showers and baths are second. They use 20 percent.

Save The Water Outside

✓ 💧 Use a soaker hose instead of a lawn sprinkler. Water lawns in the evening or early morning. This will reduce evaporation.

✓ 💧 Sweep sidewalks and driveways. Don't wash them down with a garden hose. You'll save lots of water.

💧 Wash your car at home. It takes less water than at a car wash. A trigger nozzle on the hose helps. It will save another 20 gallons (75 liters) of water each time.

💧 Avoid using lawn chemicals. Leave the grass clippings on the lawn for natural fertilizer. Then supplement it with *organic* fertilizers.

Did You Know...

You'll save lots of water by sweeping the sidewalks instead of washing them down with a garden hose.

Save The Water at School

Ask your school to install low-flow shower heads. Ask them to put in faucet *aerators*. Low-flow shower heads reduce water consumption by 50 percent.

Urge your school to use organic lawn care methods. The poisons used on lawns can make people and animals sick.

Work with your classmates to write letters to lawmakers. Urge your lawmakers to pass stricter clean water laws.

Turn The Tides

Before reading this book, you may have thought our supply of water was never ending. As you've found out, however, there is a limited supply of water on the Earth. As more people realize this fact, they are doing more things to protect our most precious natural resource.

This book is full of helpful hints on how to conserve water. If you follow even a few of these suggestions, you will save hundreds of gallons of water a year. Encourage others to follow your example. By conserving water now, you'll make sure that there will be plenty of clean water for your children and grandchildren.

Glossary

Aerators — A small device for your faucet designed to conserve water.

Aquifers — A layer or rock, sand or gravel in the Earth that holds water.

Bacteria — Very tiny plants that can only be seen through a powerful microscope.

Birth Defect — A sickness or disability with which a person is born.

Cadmium — A bluish-white metal harmful if injested by humans.

Cancer — A harmful growth in the body. It can be caused by exposure to pollution.

Conserve — To protect and wisely use forests, rivers, minerals and other natural resources.

Contaminate — To make dirty.

Drought — A long time during which there is very little or no rain.

Evaporation — To change from a liquid or solid into a gas.

Finite — Limited.

Fertilizer — Material added to soil to provide food for plants.

Geyser — A hot spring.

Glacier — A large mass of ice that does not melt.

Groundwater — Water in the Earth that supplies wells and springs. ✓

Hazardous Waste — Waste that hurts people, animals or the environment. ✓

Herbicide — A chemical used to kill plants. ✓

Hot Spring — A spring with water above 98 degrees Fahrenheit (37 degrees Celsius).

Landfill — An area built up by burying layers of trash between layers of dirt. ✓

Latex — A kind of paint that can be cleaned with water.

Lead — A heavy bluish-white metal harmful to humans.

Miscarriage — When a woman loses a baby before it's born.

Mercury — A heavy silver-colored metal harmful to humans.

Organic — Having to do with or coming from living things.

Outfall — The mouth of a body of water, a drain or a sewer.

Pesticide — A chemical used to kill bugs and other pests. ✓

Phosphate — A poisonous chemical element.

Pollution — Harming the environment by putting man-made ✓ wastes in the air, water and ground.

Recycle — Reusing materials instead of throwing them away. ✓

Sediment — Small pieces of material that settle at the bottom of a liquid.

Toxic — Something poisonous. ✓

Volcano — An opening in the surface of the Earth. Molten rock, gasses and ashes come out of the surface.

Wetlands — Land or areas that contain much soil moisture. ✓

Index

TARGET EARTH™ COMMITMENT

At Target, we're committed to the environment. We show this commitment not only through our own internal efforts but also through the programs we sponsor in the communities where we do business.

Our commitment to children and the environment began when we became the Founding International Sponsor for Kids for Saving Earth, a non-profit environmental organization for kids. We helped launch the program in 1989 and supported its growth to three-quarters of a million club members in just three years.

Our commitment to children's environmental education led to the development of an environmental curriculum called Target Earth™, aimed at getting kids involved in their education and in their world.

In addition, we worked with Abdo & Daughters Publishing to develop the Target Earth™ Earthmobile, an environmental science library on wheels that can be used in libraries, or rolled from classroom to classroom.

Target believes that the children are our future and the future of our planet. Through education, they will save the world!

TARGET®

Minneapolis-based Target Stores is an upscale discount department store chain of 517 stores in 33 states coast-to-coast, and is the largest division of Dayton Hudson Corporation, one of the nation's leading retailers.